THE ART OF JAPANESE LIVING

THE ART OF JAPANESE LIVING

Text by Claire Berrisford

An Hachette UK Company
www.hachette.co.uk

Summersdale Publishers Ltd
Part of Octopus Publishing Group Limited
Carmelite House
50 Victoria Embankment
LONDON
EC4Y 0DZ
UK

www.summersdale.com

Printed and bound in the Czech Republic

ISBN: 978-1-78783-030-1

Substantial discounts on bulk quantities of Summersdale books are available to corporations, professional associations and other organizations. For details contact general enquiries: telephone: +44 (0) 1243 771107 or email: enquiries@summersdale.com.

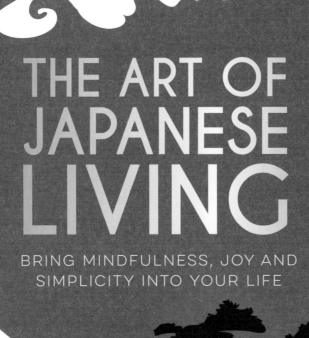

THE ART OF JAPANESE LIVING

BRING MINDFULNESS, JOY AND SIMPLICITY INTO YOUR LIFE

JO PETERS

summersdale

CONCEPTS FOR LIVING

CONTENTS

HOME LIFE

INTRODUCTION

Japanese culture is known for its sincere and thoughtful approach to life. From small day-to-day routines to ancient traditions such as the tea ceremony, the Japanese way of living shows us that in every corner of the day there is room for a moment of mindfulness.

In a world that's constantly speeding up, there is much we can learn from the Japanese attitude to life. With its roots in Buddhist thinking, the culture has a lot to say about the positive power of gratitude; about the vital connection between nature and our well-being; and about the value of a calm and considered approach to the everyday.

You can find all these things and more inside this beautiful volume. Take a step into the meditative arts of bonsai, *ikebana* and origami, or try your hand at cooking some delicious Japanese dishes. Rediscover the restorative wonders of a hot bath, be inspired by the philosophy of the tea ceremony, or bring stillness to your heart with forest bathing. See the world through a new lens with *wabi sabi*, or discover value and beauty in imperfection with *kintsugi*.

Within these pages lie the secrets to everyday contentment and the key to living a rich, joyful and thoughtful life. There are many ways that we can be inspired by Japanese culture to find peace and happiness, and this book will show you how.

生き甲斐

Ikigai

Finding what gives you a meaningful life

YOUR *IKIGAI*

We all want a sense of purpose in our lives – something that makes us happy and makes our lives feel full; something that spurs us on to get out of bed in the morning. The Japanese have a word for this feeling of purpose: *ikigai*, which translates roughly as "a reason for living". It's a core belief or feeling that characterizes who you are and what's most important to you, and many believe that finding and defining your *ikigai* – the thing that makes you tick – is the key to feeling fulfilled and happy.

Your *ikigai* is a current that runs through your whole life. However, although it sounds grand, the actions you take to pursue it often play out on the small-scale – your *ikigai* will inform the simple transactions of day-to-day life. For instance, if your *ikigai* was to help other people, holding the door open for someone could be a small everyday way of pursuing what makes you feel happiest.

Your *ikigai* will be unique to you, because we all find happiness in different ways. You may find it through your work, or through a hobby. Your *ikigai* could be providing and caring for your family, or you could find it through creating beauty, by making laughter, or by spreading peace. You may even find

that your *ikigai* changes as you go through life, because what brings you joy at 25 may be different to what fulfils you at 65.

Finding your *ikigai* is not something that happens overnight. Being able to boil your life's purpose down to one sentence requires self-reflection and insight, and it means being completely in tune with yourself. Even if you have an approximate sense of what your *ikigai* might be, it can take years before you reach a conclusion.

You probably have a good idea of what you like and don't like doing, but your *ikigai* runs deeper than having a passion for something. For instance, you may be a keen gardener, but ask yourself *why* you love gardening. Why does it bring you joy and satisfaction? Is it because you like seeing the continual progress of the plants that you tend to? Is it because you want to cultivate beautiful things? Is it because you like to create order and structure? Once you have answered this question, think about it in terms of your life as a whole. Do you enjoy finding beauty, structure or progress in other areas of your life too? Once you start looking, it is likely that you will start to see patterns in your answers. This is the start of finding your *ikigai*.

WHAT IT IS AND WHAT IT ISN'T

Primarily, your *ikigai* should be something that brings you joy and leaves you feeling fulfilled rather than drained. Even if your *ikigai* is related to making others happy, it should also make *you* happy; it won't be something you do out of a sense of obligation.

Your *ikigai* will usually help you connect to the people around you, as it's often about what you can give to the world rather than what you can take. For instance, a writer's work will be read and discussed, an artist's work will be viewed and a volunteer's time will help another person. An *ikigai* will also be active – not passive. It's something that you deliberately pursue for the specific purpose of bringing you joy, even if it's as simple as going for a walk, reading a book or talking to a friend.

Your *ikigai* is often related to things you can see growing and developing, whether you're working on a project, improving a skill or watching a child growing up. This is also why an *ikigai* will not be a specific goal. Your *ikigai* is a defining part of your self that will always be with you, so there is no finish line. However, it doesn't mean that your *ikigai* can't help you achieve your dreams. For instance, your *ikigai* would not be to publish a novel, but it could be sharing stories and connecting with others. In that case, publishing a novel might be something you do in the course of pursuing your purpose.

THE GIFTS OF *IKIGAI*

So why bother identifying your *ikigai*? It takes so much time and effort – why not just carry on through life doing the things you like to do and avoiding the things you don't? Because having a concrete grasp on what makes you *you* – a definite sentence that defines who you are and what your purpose is – is empowering.

Knowing your *ikigai* means that you have a deep understanding of yourself and what makes you feel your best. It means you know how to find happiness. It also gives you a sense of control, it helps you direct your life and it enables you to pinpoint what motivates you.

Your *ikigai* is also an anchor, and it can help to guide you in times of difficulty, because you know with certainty what matters to you and what your priorities are.

Studies show that understanding your *ikigai* can help you to live longer too – this is most likely because it helps to keep your mind and body active, it maintains your positivity and drive for life, and it helps to keep you connected to those around you.

HOW TO FIND YOUR *IKIGAI*

Finding your *ikigai* can take many years, and people often find that it reveals itself over time, rather than being found. However, there are ways you can help to kickstart this process of self-discovery.

Start by asking questions. What moments do you most enjoy in everyday life? What do you do without anyone asking you to do? What were your favourite things to do as a child? What makes you feel emotions strongly? What are you looking forward to? If money was no object, what would you still want to do? The answers to these kinds of questions will give you a feel for what makes you tick; the next step is to look at your answers and see if you can find patterns.

The key is to pay attention to yourself and the way you feel. Notice when you are curious about something and allow yourself to follow it. Interrogate your hobbies – why do you love doing what you do? Although your *ikigai* is more than a passion, our hobbies tell us a lot about what we feel deeply within ourselves.

Don't feel you have to search too far beyond yourself and the life you already live. You will probably naturally have a sense of what your *ikigai* might be, as you will already know what inspires and draws your attention. It just takes time to be able to crystallize those feelings into a single sentence. And, while you're taking that time, remember that, even if you don't have your *ikigai* defined completely, every day spent paying attention to what inspires you and brings you joy will help you to live a richer, more fulfilled life.

Essentials to happiness in this life are something to do, something to love, and something to hope for.

Hector Garcia

侘寂

Wabi sabi

Seeing beauty in imperfection,
and accepting that life is transient

WHAT IS *WABI SABI?*

Wabi sabi is an enigma of Japanese culture. It's not something that people tend to learn or discuss, and there is no dictionary definition for the term: it is, essentially, undefinable. *Wabi sabi* is a concept that's simply understood, and it is ubiquitous, underpinning many aspects of Japanese culture, from art to architecture to everyday life.

In broad terms, *wabi sabi* is an aesthetic principle – a way of seeing and understanding beauty in the world – which embraces imperfection and transience. Perhaps one way to explain it is in contrast: whereas Western ideals of beauty emphasize perfection and longevity, *wabi sabi* favours incompleteness and impermanence.

We can gain an understanding of the concept through each individual word. Over time, *wabi* has come to denote simple, rustic beauty, quietude and stillness. For instance, *wabi* qualities can be found in minimal interiors, in frugality and in periods of solitude in nature. *Sabi* is about finding beauty and character in objects that show marks of age and experience – it can be seen in the spine of a book cracked from being opened many times, or in a tree which is gnarled in old age.

When the words are combined, the term *wabi sabi* is about how *you* personally perceive and understand the kinds of beauty connoted by each word. Although there is no specific definition, at its core *wabi sabi* is about finding beauty in imperfection; about accepting that all things in life are transient and always changing; and it's about the very act of feeling these things and the peace and contentment that it can bring.

Every person's experience of *wabi sabi* will be unique to them, because we all find beauty in different things. But what is universal is that *wabi sabi* is a moment of deep appreciation – a way of experiencing the world from your heart. And it's this deep appreciation that can give us a sense of tranquillity and contentment.

WABI SABI
AND BUDDHISM

The philosophy of *wabi sabi* is deeply connected to Buddhism. Buddhism teaches that there are three characteristics, of existence: impermanence, suffering and the idea that there is no permanent and unchanging self, and that wisdom lies in being able to accept these three things.

Wabi sabi is said to be a way of embodying these teachings. By understanding that transience is the world's natural state, and finding beauty within this, we can begin to accept impermanence. Finding beauty in objects that show age and marks of use is a way to accept suffering. By coming to terms with the fact that we ourselves are also fluid and changing – always incomplete and always imperfect – we can begin to accept that there is no such thing as a definitive or tangible "self". Therefore, *wabi sabi* not only helps us to understand the way we exist in the world – it also allows us to find a sense of truth and peace within it.

Because life is full of uncertainty, one must engrave in his heart the events of the day as if there is no tomorrow.

SEN NO RIKYŪ

EXPERIENCING *WABI SABI*

Wabi sabi means finding beauty in the things that are simple, rustic and humble, and in the things that draw attention to their history, or their connection to nature. Although every experience of *wabi sabi* will be unique, here are a few examples of things that commonly inspire that moment of appreciation and deep feeling:

THE SEASONS

Seeing leaves change in autumn from green to golden yellows and reds means that they will soon fall, which reminds us that life is always changing and moving onward. Therefore, the present moment is something to cherish, because it is fleeting.

NATURE

Nature will always leave its mark. Rock will become weather-beaten and adorned with lichen, moss will grow between cracks in paving stones. Roots of trees can disrupt the structures that we build. Each time we notice these ways that nature affects the world, it is another reminder that change is the world's natural state, and that nothing will last.

POSSESSIONS

The marks of use on our possessions tell stories about us and about the lives that the objects have lived with us. A loved cuddly toy will be threadbare from all the attention it has received over its life. A stain on a tablecloth will always carry the memories of the day the stain was made and will remind you of the time that has passed since. An object may even have a new purpose – a used wine bottle could be a candleholder, for instance. Every time it is used we will be aware of its history.

PEOPLE AND RELATIONSHIPS

Wabi sabi can change how we see our relationships with others and can help us to value them more highly. Relationships will naturally ebb and flow, and they won't always remain the same, so enjoy the time that you have right now and cherish the happy moments that you have.

THE LESSONS OF *WABI SABI*

Wabi sabi can help to change the way we view the world and how we understand our place in it. In turn, this can lead us toward moments of joy, happiness and contentment.

SELF-ACCEPTANCE

We can accept ourselves and all our quirks because we are imperfect. "Imperfect" is not a negative term: it is simply a truthful and descriptive one. It denotes that things are always growing and changing, and it acknowledges that we are only ever now, not yesterday or tomorrow.

LETTING GO OF PERFECT

Whatever you are striving to improve – your career, your home, your image – let go of perfect. Perfection is an impossible state to reach, because it implies that something is finished, when nothing ever is. Life will always be imperfect.

THE HABIT OF JOY

Once you start to see beauty in the world around you, it becomes a habit. You will be attuned to moments of joy and fully able to take notice of them. Being able to appreciate these small moments helps you to feel gratitude for where you are and see the world in a more positive light.

A NEW OUTLOOK

Nothing is permanent, not even failure or disappointment. *Wabi sabi* helps us to reframe failure as something that has happened but also something that we can move on from, rather than it being a weight that will drag you down forever.

RESILIENCE

Wabi sabi helps us to be resilient. If we are able to accept that things change, then we will be less shocked when they do. You will be able to take change in your stride, instead of letting it knock you down.

LIVING FOR NOW

Whether we like it or not, the past is gone. The events that have happened make us the people we are, but those moments no longer exist. Live in the moment; focus on where you are right now and enjoy your life as it happens.

The bamboo shoot that
bends is stronger than
the oak that resists.

Japanese proverb

物
の
哀
れ

MONO NO AWARE

[moh-noh-noh-AH-wah-reh]

A deep, wistful, bittersweet feeling, often inspired by fleeting beauty. Cherry blossoms or sunsets often evoke a sense of mono no aware: *they are beautiful, but a part of their beauty is because of how short-lived they are. The term roughly translates to "the pathos of things" or "the ahhh-ness of things".*

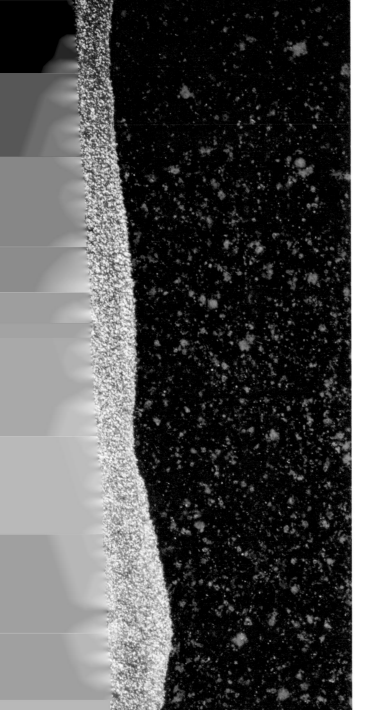

金継ぎ

Kintsugi

Repairing broken pottery with gold

KINTSUGI

Kintsugi, meaning "golden joinery", refers to the art of repairing broken pottery with gold-dusted lacquer – the idea being that the object becomes more beautiful for having broken and been put back together.

The technique can be subtle or striking, depending entirely on how the piece of pottery has broken. Sometimes just a small chip in the side of a bowl or plate will be filled in, which is only noticeable if you look closely. Sometimes, the entire vessel can be shot through with veins of gold, which show the dramatic starbursts of fault lines and the zigzags where fragmented edges used to be. No two repairs will be the same.

Legend tells that *kintsugi* began in the fifteenth century, when the shogun of Japan, Ashikaga Yoshimasa, sent a broken tea bowl back to China to be repaired. When it arrived back, it had been put back together with staples, as was the custom at the time for ceramics. The unsightly nature of the staples displeased him, so a new way was sought to repair pottery. The shogun's cup was mended again by filling its cracks with lacquered resin and powdered gold, and so *kintsugi* was born.

In *kintsugi,* the act of repair is really an act of rebirth. Instead of trying to return a cup to its former state, it is transformed into a treasure. The lustre of the gold draws attention to its fracture lines and flaws, so they are not hidden but celebrated. They give the cup history and memory; they show that the object is loved and respected; and they make it unique and irreplaceable. It becomes a symbol of transience, strength and beauty.

A cup or bowl repaired with *kintsugi* is also a living demonstration of *wabi sabi* – the idea that imperfection is beautiful and that change is something to be accepted and embraced.

The world breaks everyone and afterward many are strong at the broken places.

Ernest Hemingway

KINTSUGI FOR OUR SELVES

Kintsugi may be primarily about repairing pottery, but the philosophy behind it holds many empowering messages for our own lives.

EMBRACE YOUR FLAWS

The way the gold accentuates the cracks in a pot reminds us to celebrate what makes us different. No two people are the same – nobody looks the same, thinks the same or has had the same experiences as any other person – which makes each of us unique and irreplaceable. Whether they are external or internal, what we may consider to be flaws, marks or traits that make us stand out are what make us individuals. So don't cover them up! Embrace your quirks and love them for making you you.

CHANGE IS A PART OF LIFE

Kintsugi also reminds us that change is an inevitable part of life and that who we are is always changing too. Instead of clinging to an ideal of who we should be, or who we have been, we should simply accept who we are in this moment. We are not fixed in time, and we are never either whole or broken. We are simply changing, from one moment to the next. Life will always leave its marks but,

just like the pots covered with gold, these marks are our history, and they show us how we've grown.

YOU ARE STRONG

The philosophy of *kintsugi* also encourages us to think differently about hardships. We will all face adversity at some time in our lives, but, even if we feel broken, we can rebuild – and our characters will always be stronger for having done so. Being able to rebuild doesn't mean having to forget our past experiences, but it means accepting them as part of us and being strong enough to move on from them.

BE KIND TO YOURSELF

Perhaps most importantly, *kintsugi* reminds us of the importance of loving ourselves. A broken cup cannot be fixed on its own; it requires love, care and attention before it can become whole again – and we are the same. When we experience hardship, it is care, kindness and time that will put us and those around us back together.

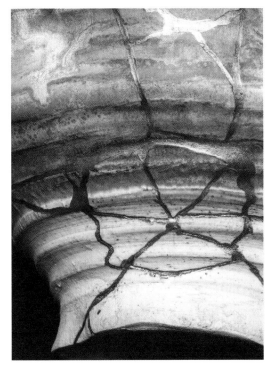

KINTSUGI IN THE HOME

Although the art of *kintsugi* refers to ceramics, the mindset can be applied much more broadly to our belongings and best-loved possessions. The holes in a favourite jumper or pair of trousers could be mended with a colourful patch of material. A missing zip pull could be replaced with a beautifully plaited piece of string. Drawers or doors with broken handles could be given new life with decorative knobs, in whatever style you feel represents you. Just like in *kintsugi*, each item is given new life, and the way it is repaired celebrates the change rather than hides it.

Present in every *kintsugi*-like repair is the concept of *wabi sabi*, the idea that life is in a constant state of change, helping us to accept that what might, at first, seem like an ending is not necessarily the end. For instance, something we own might be "imperfect", because its condition has changed over time. But this belonging is more beautiful, and much more our own, because we have history with it, and it tells a story – both of the object and the love of the owner.

I can be
changed by what
happens to me.
But I refuse to
be reduced by it.

MAYA ANGELOU

The wound is where
the light enters you.

Rumi

桜梅桃李

OUBAITORI

[O-bai-toe-ree]

Everybody is different and should value their own unique traits – the same way that cherry, apricot, peach and plum trees are different but are all beautiful and have their own purpose.

森林浴

Shinrin-yoku

Forest bathing

WHAT IS *SHINRIN-YOKU?*

Shinrin-yoku is a therapeutic pastime more commonly known in the West by its English translation, forest bathing. The practice originated in Japan in the 1980s, after the government heavily invested in a nationwide program to promote health and well-being. Since then it has only gained in popularity, and this form of therapy is being adopted across the world. Contrary to its name, forest bathing has nothing to do with wallowing in water surrounded by trees. More literally, it's the act of being among trees, absorbing the ambience of a forest.

This kind of therapy is a balm for the body and mind. Modern life dictates that we spend much of our time inside, but in reality, we are not programmed for this sort of lifestyle. Urban environments surround us with all kinds of stimuli that lead to a huge amount of stress on our minds and bodies. The relentless exposure to technology, and the expectation that we should be constantly digitally connected and available, adds further pressure. Taking time to be among trees, and to engage with the great outdoors, gives us the connection to nature that we so desperately need. Escaping to the forest is the natural antidote, and it helps our bodies and minds to rest and be restored.

THE AMAZING POWER OF *SHINRIN-YOKU*

The practice of forest bathing is scientifically proven to improve our overall well-being. Studies show that after only a short amount of time in the arbour of a forest, stress levels are reduced. Walking among trees decreases the body's stress response, which, in turn, lowers your levels of cortisol, the stress hormone. This also contributes to lowering your heart rate and blood pressure; as a result, you feel calmer and your body is healthier. It is also thought that the quiet atmosphere, beautiful scenery and temperate climate often found in forests all contribute to this sense of wellness.

Forest bathing also offers a free aromatherapy session. Natural essential oils, known as phytoncides, are emitted by trees to protect themselves from germs and insects, and they have a positive impact on humans too by naturally boosting our immune systems.

木漏れ日

KOMOREBI

[koh-moh-reh-bee]

*Sunlight filtering through
the leaves of the trees.*

HOW TO FOREST BATHE

A forest is a place of stillness and calm, somewhere the noise and bustle of daily life can't quite reach. It's a peaceful, natural space where you can unwind, refresh and restore yourself. In a world where we are constantly pressured to do more and be more, forest bathing is the art of "not doing".

Begin by simply walking through the forest. Take your time and go slowly. Notice where you are putting your feet, feel the ground beneath you and be aware of the trees stretching out beside, ahead of and above you.

Use all your senses to absorb the atmosphere: the sunlight, and all the different shades of green, brown or orange. Notice the small details about your surroundings – flowers or mushrooms growing on the forest floor or how roots have grown and twisted over rocks. Take note of how the forest makes you feel in your heart, the emotions it brings and the thoughts that it inspires within you.

Feel the texture of bark and the veins on the undersides of leaves. Hear the birdsong, or the sound of the wind rustling the leaves, or maybe even rain pattering onto the canopy above. Smell the scent of the earth.

Breath the clean air. Take slow, full breaths as you walk. Stop if you want to and sit beneath a tree. Deepen your breathing – inhale through your nose for four counts, hold for four, then breathe out for seven counts, and repeat.

Stay quiet as you bathe. There is no need to talk and no pressure to do anything. This is time for you to simply be.

YŪGEN

As you gaze up into the leaves of the trees and begin to truly immerse yourself in your surroundings, forest bathing may inspire a moment of *yūgen*. The word refers to a feeling that's often too deep or complex to explain.

Similar to the deep appreciation of *wabi sabi, yūgen* allows you to experience the present moment deeply and to feel connection with the world around you on a profound level. When you are struck by *yūgen*, you will also feel a sense of wonder: a feeling that hints at hidden depths of the world and suggests that you are part of something much larger than yourself.

The clearest way into
the universe is through
a forest wilderness.

John Muir

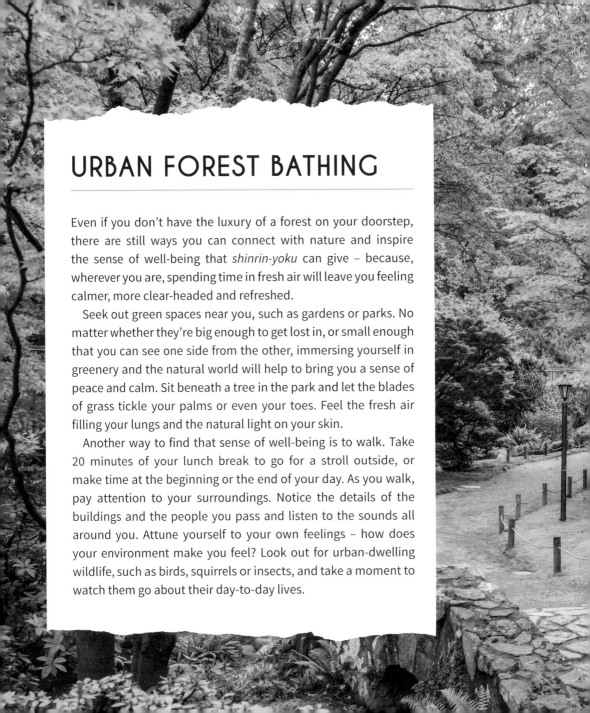

URBAN FOREST BATHING

Even if you don't have the luxury of a forest on your doorstep, there are still ways you can connect with nature and inspire the sense of well-being that *shinrin-yoku* can give – because, wherever you are, spending time in fresh air will leave you feeling calmer, more clear-headed and refreshed.

Seek out green spaces near you, such as gardens or parks. No matter whether they're big enough to get lost in, or small enough that you can see one side from the other, immersing yourself in greenery and the natural world will help to bring you a sense of peace and calm. Sit beneath a tree in the park and let the blades of grass tickle your palms or even your toes. Feel the fresh air filling your lungs and the natural light on your skin.

Another way to find that sense of well-being is to walk. Take 20 minutes of your lunch break to go for a stroll outside, or make time at the beginning or the end of your day. As you walk, pay attention to your surroundings. Notice the details of the buildings and the people you pass and listen to the sounds all around you. Attune yourself to your own feelings – how does your environment make you feel? Look out for urban-dwelling wildlife, such as birds, squirrels or insects, and take a moment to watch them go about their day-to-day lives.

おもてなし

Omotenashi

Selfless, genuine hospitality

OMOTENASHI

Japan is preceded by its reputation for outstanding customer service and hospitality. Even in rush hour, cleaners bow to passengers on bullet trains, and, whether you are setting foot in a five-star hotel, a local restaurant, or even a small corner shop, you will always be greeted by calls of *"irasshaimase"*, which equates to a combination of "welcome" and "come in".

This hospitality is known as *omotenashi*, the desire to make others comfortable, whether they are customers, guests, clients or friends. However, it runs deeper than being polite – it's a selfless and genuine hospitality that is given without expecting anything in return, and it's present in all moments of everyday life, from high-powered business interactions to informal social settings.

We can understand the concept more by looking at the word itself: *"omote"* is what you present to the outside world – your public face – and *"nashi"* means "nothing" or "less". When the words are combined, they come to mean "single-hearted": the idea that the face you present to others is completely genuine and nothing is hidden. In other words, the hospitality that you are showing to the people around you is sincere and comes from the heart.

THE HOSPITALITY OF TEA

The concept of *omotenashi* is firmly rooted in Japan's cultural history and originates from the tea ceremony. At its heart, the tea ceremony is an elaborate offering of hospitality, and it aims to create a harmonious atmosphere between the people who have gathered together. *Omotenashi* is the way that this principle plays out in the wider world; each act of service sparks a moment of happiness and connection in an otherwise busy life and goes a long way to creating a sense of harmony between yourself and others.

One kind word can warm
three winter months.

Japanese proverb

SPREAD A LITTLE KINDNESS

The concept of *omotenashi* is an inspiring example of how both our lives and the lives of the people around us can be improved with simple acts of kindness. Tucked away in the everyday are so many opportunities to create moments of harmony through being sensitive to the needs of others.

Hospitality can be shown in a literal sense – by holding the door for someone, by offering to carry a heavy bag, by being willing to share what you have and by offering to help people if you see that they need it, even if it means going out of your way.

But it doesn't have to be so overt. Hospitality can be subtle; for instance, if you are having a conversation, really listen to your partner and give them your full attention. Giving people the benefit of the doubt is another example. This kindness may not always be felt by others immediately, but interacting with people without judgement will make them feel welcome and both of you will be more comfortable.

Equally, try to notice when people have gone out of their way for you – whether someone has helped you with a chore, offered you advice or helped you out with a problem – and thank them for it. Not only will they appreciate your thanks, but practising this kind of gratitude helps you to become attuned to the small moments of happiness that can be found in the everyday.

Living life with an outlook of kindness and consideration is one of the simplest ways we can bring harmony to the world around us. It also adds a richness and happiness to our own lives, because when you lift someone up, it lifts you up too.

Even the smallest kindness will not be forgotten.

Japanese proverb

御馳走様 でした

GOCHISOUSAMA-DESHITA

(goh-chih-SOH-sama-DE-shTA)

The phrase that is said at the end of a meal to express your thanks for the trouble that the host and cook have gone to in preparing it; equivalent to saying, "Thank you for the nice meal."

"THANKS TO YOU..."

Gratitude is also built into the Japanese language. A good example is the phrase *"okagesamade"*, which is a way of saying thank you in casual conversation. The word translates roughly as "thanks to you" or "thanks to your support", and it's used as a humble way to acknowledge all the help that you receive from the world. For instance, if someone asked, "How are you?", you might respond, "Fine, thanks to you." This way, you acknowledge any assistance that you may have had to get to where you are today, whether you are aware of it or not.

Alternatively, someone may comment that you are good at something. For example, "You're a great cook!" A good response would be to use *"okagesamade"*; you may have a natural talent for food, but you also have a kitchen to work in, equipment that you use, money to buy ingredients, people who have taught you, cooking techniques that have been developed over hundreds of years of human history... The list could be endless. By saying *okagesamade*, you show that you are grateful for all the unseen forces that act on a situation and allow you to be where you are.

家

Ie

The Japanese home

THE JAPANESE HOME

The traditional Japanese home is perhaps the area with the most pronounced difference to the Western way of living. Instead of carpets, hinged doors and concrete walls and floors, you might find *tatami* mats on the floors and sliding doors made of paper (*shōji* and *fusuma*). In the living room space there may be a low table (*chabudai*) surrounded by cushions to sit on (*zabuton*). Instead of beds, futons are often favoured. The decor is typically minimal and understated, free from clutter and focused on muted colours and natural materials.

However, despite the differences, a home is your sanctuary, no matter where you are in the world. It's the place you return to at the end of the day to relax, to spend time with your family and to be yourself. There are many elements about the Japanese way of living that we can take inspiration from, and we can use these ideas to create spaces where we can express ourselves and feel relaxed and happy.

OUTSIDE AND INSIDE

Japanese homes take care to separate the outside world from the inside world, and one of the main ways to achieve this is built into the house itself.

The *genkan* is the Japanese equivalent to a hallway – a small porch-like area which is usually lower than the floor level of the house. In this area you would take off your shoes before proceeding into the home. The fact that you wouldn't ever walk in or out without this moment of pause means that your home and the outside world always remain a little apart from each other. Many Japanese people also wash their hands and gargle water on arriving home to cleanse themselves of impurities from the outside world, or they will change out of their work clothes and into something more comfortable before settling into the evening. This all contributes to a sense of difference between "home" and the world outside.

One major contributor to our rising stress levels is the feeling that we cannot relax and switch off, even when we return home at the end of a busy day. However, making clear distinctions between home and the outside world can help you to change tack and begin to unwind.

おじゃまします

OJAMASHIMASU

(OH-jah-mah-shi-mass)

Translating as "I am sorry for your trouble" or "I am disturbing you", this is a polite greeting to use when you enter someone's home and acknowledges that you are imposing on them.

TRANSFORM YOUR SPACE

In Japan, space is a precious resource. As a result, there is a fluidity to Japanese homes, and their interiors have the ability to transform. The main area of the home is often more of a "space" than a room, as it can be adapted to suit many purposes, becoming a bedroom, dining room, meditation space or study as needed. The sliding partitions between the rooms can create more or less space. Futons are tidied away during the day, and sometimes even furniture, such as low tables, can be stored, leaving a large area of space free for activities, family time or receiving guests.

Although you can't move the walls in most Western homes, there are still ways you can make the space you have work hard for you. Consider investing in a room divider so that you can zone different spaces in your home. For instance, if your living room has a table as well as a sofa area, use the divider to partition the room into two spaces: one for studying and the other for relaxing. You could also place it around your clothes racks as you dry your laundry which will contain it in its own area and make the rest of your space feel tidier and less cluttered.

Furniture that can perform multiple functions is another simple way to make your space more flexible. A sofa bed is a good example, as is a lidded foot stool that can be used as an extra seat if you have guests, with the added benefit of having room inside it to store living room items to make your space tidier.

MINIMAL AND CLUTTER FREE

Whether it's because they're small city apartments with limited space, or whether they are aiming for a *wabi-sabi* aesthetic, Japanese homes tend to be minimal in style and free from clutter. Every item in the home will have a purpose and a place in this streamlined approach to living.

Having a tidy and organized space to come home to has a huge effect on our mood and our outlook on life. Not only does it help us to feel more in control, but it's far easier to relax in a space that is tidy. Decluttering also has the benefit of making us focus on what matters to us by stripping away the things we don't need.

HOW TO DECLUTTER

Decluttering can seem like a daunting task, but it needn't be if you take it one step at a time. First, pick an area of your home. It could be your wardrobe, a bits-and-bobs drawer in the kitchen, a pile of paperwork, or even your sock drawer. Then go through the items, sorting them into piles to keep, throw away or rehome. Be realistic as you sort through and ask yourself if you really need each item.

TINY TIDY MOMENTS

Although decluttering is a great way to tidy your home, no matter how thoroughly you do it there will always be little things that you can't get rid of but that are also hard to keep presentable. Here are a few simple storage tricks to help you create a more organized home.

BEDROOM

Repurpose an ice-cube tray and use the wells to keep your jewellery organized and easy to access.

DESK

Organize your desk drawers by making dividers out of cereal boxes. Simply draw a line around the bottom of the box the same depth as your drawer, then cut. You should be left with a small rectangular tray. Make as many as will fit in your drawer. You can then use them to organize your stationery and other desk items.

KITCHEN

Use a glass jar or cookie jar to store the necessary bits and bobs that would otherwise hang around the kitchen and dining room area, such as pens, post-its, elastic bands or pegs.

BATHROOM

Hook a waterproof hanging basket in the shower to keep your soaps and shampoos organized and out of the way.

KEEP IT NATURAL

Natural materials feature heavily in traditional Japanese homes, from the interiors, with the paper *shōji* screens and the *tatami* mats woven from rushes, right down to their very structures, which are made from wood. Although modern Japanese homes are now more commonly built with concrete, they still tend to embrace the natural world in their décor, and furniture, ornaments and items around the home will often be made from organic materials. This manner of decoration contributes to a *wabi-sabi* aesthetic, as it brings beauty to the home in the form of simple, humble and natural materials that will, eventually, weather with age.

As well as providing a home with a *wabi-sabi*-inspired beauty, bringing the outside in, in all its forms, brings a room to life and makes us feel good. Think about choosing wooden ornaments or a plain wooden photo frame, keeping a pot plant or using wicker baskets as storage. When choosing materials, look for natural fabrics with plenty of texture like cotton, linen, hemp or wool. You could also add a mirror to a room to help make the most of the natural light and clean your windows to make sure as much light as possible is getting in.

故郷

FURUSATO

(foo-roo-sah-toh)

A word to refer to your home town, which is layered with a sense of nostalgia. The word implies that furusato is not just where you come from, it's where your heart calls home too.

もったいない

Mottainai

Appreciating the value of
everyday objects

MOTTAINAI!

If you were to eat a portion of rice in Japan and leave a few grains lingering in the bottom of the bowl, you might be met with the exclamation *"Mottainai!"* Something similar might be said if you threw something away instead of mending it, or if you got rid of an item when it still had life left.

Mottainai is a way to express regret that something has been wasted, whether it's food, clothing or items around your home. It can be used both as an exclamation – "What a waste!" – and as a word of advice – "Don't be wasteful."

The regret in *mottainai* stems from the belief that the items we have are precious and deserve respect – to waste them means that their full potential has not been reached, or that their intrinsic value has not been properly appreciated. Instead, by reusing items, repairing them and recycling them, we treat them with the respect they deserve.

REDUCE, REUSE, RECYCLE

The spirit of *mottainai* encourages us to treasure the things that we have and to make the most of them, whether that's by finishing all the food on your plate, mending the things that break, repurposing objects or finding a new home for them.

Implicit in the word is also the advice that we take care of our belongings so that they last a long time and that we don't introduce any more waste into the world than is necessary. In a time where our seas are full of plastic and the environment is contaminated with litter and debris, this message is more important than ever.

The natural world is changing...
It is the most precious thing we
have and we need to defend it.

David Attenborough

THERE ARE MANY EASY WAYS THAT WE CAN REUSE AND RECYCLE IN OUR DAY-TO-DAY LIVES:

- Egg shells can be scattered on your garden as a natural waste-free slug and snail repellent. Coffee grounds can also be distributed to help nourish your soil.

- Save citrus fruit peel to add to your bath. The hot water brings out the essential oils, so you can enjoy a spa experience for free.

- Some items that we tend to think of as single-use can be used multiple times: kitchen foil can be unfolded and reused, sandwich bags can be washed and margarine tubs can be used as containers for the freezer.

- Old T-shirts can be used as cleaning rags and dusters, or as an alternative to bubble wrap if you are posting or moving breakable items. If you like being creative, they can be braided together to make rugs or bath mats – tutorials for these can be found online.

- A mesh fruit/vegetable bag can be scrunched up and used as a scrubber in the kitchen.

- A used tea bag can be turned into a bin freshener; wait until it's dry, add a few drops of essential oil and place at the bottom of the bin.

- Used tea bags can also be used to shine mirrors. Take a wet (but not dripping) tea bag and wipe your mirror. Then buff it with a soft cloth using circular motions to make the glass shine.

- Glass jars can be used to store dry goods – such as rice, sugar, flour or salt – in the cupboard and leftover food or sauce in the fridge, or they can be turned into pen pots, small planters or handy containers for string or twine.

- Old toothbrushes can be demoted to household cleaning duty and be used to clean delicate or intricate items.

FUROSHIKI

Millions of tonnes of wrapping paper ends up in landfill sites every year. Designed for only a single use and often coated with a layer of plastic, it's a serious culprit in the contamination of planet earth. Using brown paper or newspaper is a good step toward making your gift-giving more eco-friendly, as it can be recycled. But why not go one step further and try *furoshiki*?

Furoshiki is a traditional kind of Japanese cloth. It's used to wrap all manner of objects – from clothes to lunch boxes – but it makes a particularly attractive way to present gifts. *Furoshiki* are square-shaped and often sport beautiful prints and patterns, and the finished products swathed in these cloths appear elegant and classy. Best of all, it's re-usable, so nothing is wasted.

HOW TO WRAP A BOOK OR SMALL BOX

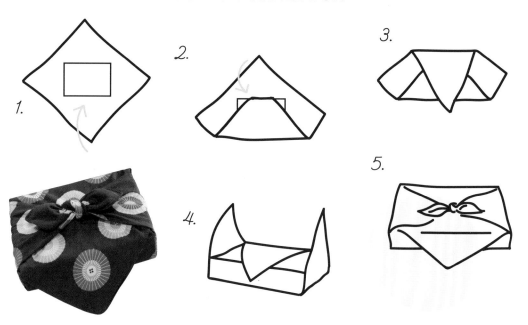

HOW TO WRAP A BOTTLE

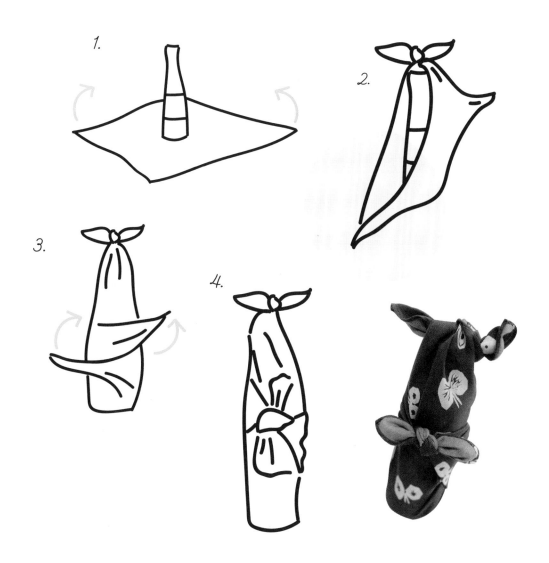

食べ物

Tabemono

Japanese food and diet

THE JAPANESE TABLE

Think of Japanese food, and any number of things may spring to mind: bowls of steaming noodles, elegant portions of sushi, fluffy white rice, fresh ingredients, colourful dishes, immaculate presentation, beautiful crockery – the list is almost endless. But not only is this cuisine world renowned for being distinctive and delicious, it's known for being one of the healthiest too.

The Japanese diet is full of fresh fruit and vegetables, grains and soy, and it contains very little saturated fat, dairy and sugar. Fermented foods also feature – such as pickled vegetables (*tsukemono*), pickled plums (*umeboshi*) and fermented soybeans, which can appear as soy sauce, tofu or miso – and are bursting with good bacteria to help promote a healthy gut.

Traditionally, steamed white rice (*gohan*) forms the base of a meal. The rice will then be accompanied by *okazu* – side dishes of vegetables, meat, fish, soup and pickles. This variety of dishes means that any Japanese meal is likely to be packed with valuable nutrients and antioxidants.

There is also significant evidence to show that the Japanese diet helps you to live longer. Japan is the country with the highest number of centenarians, and the residents of Okinawa, a group of islands south-west of Japan, have one of the highest recorded average life expectancies in the world: 82 years for men and 88 for women. Studies have concluded that, combined with close social connections and an active lifestyle, it is the traditional Japanese diet that has enabled them to achieve such longevity.

One piece of wisdom from Okinawa is *hara hachi bu*, the practice of eating until you are 80 per cent full. This way of thinking brings mindfulness to mealtimes, and it will ensure that you eat enough to be satisfied, but that you don't eat more than you need. To practise mindful eating, minimize distractions at mealtimes – focus on your food while you eat rather than looking at your phone or the TV. Try to eat more slowly, noticing every mouthful and the taste of your food, and be aware of how you feel. If you think you have satisfied your hunger but could eat a little more, you are probably 80 per cent full.

CHOPSTICK ETIQUETTE

With at least 5,000 years of history behind them, chopsticks are one of the oldest and most distinctive utensils there are, and they're easy to use once you know how. Place the lower chopstick at the base of your thumb and steady the end with your fourth finger.

It should be fixed in place. Hold the upper chopstick the same way you would hold a pencil, between your thumb and forefinger. This is the chopstick that you will manoeuvre to pick up your food.

WHEN USING CHOPSTICKS, BE MINDFUL OF THE DOS AND DON'TS:

- **Do** use a chopstick holder when you're not using your chopsticks, rather than putting them flat on the table.

- **Don't** stick your chopsticks upright in a bowl of rice, as this is reminiscent of the sticks of incense that are burned at funerals.

- **Don't** pass food from chopstick to chopstick, as this is also similar to a Buddhist funeral rite, whereby a bone is passed between members of the group. If you need to pass a piece of food, put it down on a plate, and the other person can pick it up.

- **Do** avoid being impolite: never spear your food with a chopstick, don't use them to point or gesture, and don't lick them.

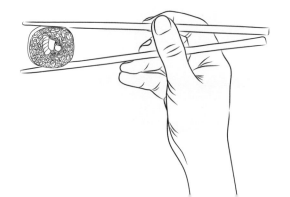

頂きます

ITADAKIMASU

(ee-tah-dah-kee-mass)

Itadakimasu is said before a meal. Although it translates as "I humbly receive", it plays a similar role to the phrases "Bon appetit" or "Let's eat!" It is a way of showing your gratitude to everybody who has had a part to play in the meal, from the cook and the host to the farmers who grew the food.

ONIGIRI

Onigiri are bite-sized balls of white rice, rolled by hand and wrapped in seaweed, and they contain a delicious savoury filling. According to archaeological finds, it's possible that these rice balls, or at least a variant of them, have been enjoyed since the first century CE and that they were developed as rations for soldiers as they were easy to transport.

Salty ingredients have traditionally been used for the fillings because in the days before refrigeration they helped to preserve the snack, and they are still used today; among the most common *onigiri* fillings are grilled salmon, tuna mayo, *umeboshi* (pickled plums), *kombu* (a type of seaweed) and bonito flakes (flakes of dried fish). Today they are a popular portable snack, whether home-made and packed in lunch boxes or bought from a convenience store.

Onigiri recipe (Makes 6)

Method

1. Wash the rice under running water for 1–2 minutes, until the draining water comes out clear. Add the rice to a pan and cover with the cold water. Leave it to soak for 30 minutes. Then put the lid on the pan and bring to the boil over a medium heat. Once boiling, reduce to a simmer for 10–12 minutes, or until all the water is absorbed. Stir occasionally. Remove the pot from the heat and allow it to steam for another 10–15 minutes with the lid on.

2. Fluff up the rice with a wooden spoon and allow it to cool with the lid off until it can be handled.

3. Cut the sheets of nori into long strips approximately 2 cm wide and put to one side.

4. Wet your hands, then rub them with a pinch of salt. Take a handful of rice (approx. 2 tbsp) and mould it into a rough ball shape in your palm. Flatten the ball, place a small amount of your chosen filling in the centre, then fold the rice over it and shape it into a ball or a triangle.

5. Take a strip of nori and wrap it around the bottom of the ball or the base of the triangle. Serve immediately, or pack into an airtight container and refrigerate until needed. Consume within two days.

for the onigiri:

225 g short-grain rice

270 ml cold water

Salt

2 sheets nori seaweed

Your choice of filling (see below)

fillings:

Umeboshi

These pickled plums can be purchased from supermarkets or online. Use a small amount of pickle per *onigiri*.

Tuna mayo

Mix half a can of tuna (approx. 40 g), 1 tbsp mayonnaise, 1 tsp light soy sauce and a pinch of sugar and salt. Adjust seasoning to taste.

Grilled salmon

In a small bowl, mix 100 g tinned salmon with a pinch of salt.

CHICKEN RAMEN *(Serves 2)*

Japanese cuisine makes the most of the fruit and vegetables that are in season, and ramen is endlessly customisable. Why not top yours with broccoli in the spring, peas and radish in the summer, grilled aubergine in the autumn or leeks in the winter?

Ingredients

150 g cooked chicken

2 tbsp sesame oil

2 tbsp light soy sauce

2 cm ginger, grated

3 large cloves garlic, chopped

1 tbsp rice wine vinegar

1 tsp sugar

450 ml chicken stock

1 tbsp miso paste

2 eggs

Handful of beansprouts

2 sheets of noodles (any kind will work)

Spring onions, chopped, to garnish

Method

1. Put the chicken in a bowl with 1 tbsp of the sesame oil and 1 tbsp light soy sauce, stir and set to one side.

2. Next, make the broth. Add the remaining sesame oil to the pan and cook the ginger and garlic until fragrant. Then add the remaining soy sauce, the rice wine vinegar and sugar. Stir to coat, then add the stock and miso paste. Bring to the boil and simmer for 10 minutes. Adjust the seasoning to taste, adding more sugar, soy sauce or sesame oil if you prefer.

3. Meanwhile, soft boil your eggs. Bring a small pan of water to the boil and cook the eggs for 5 minutes. Prepare a bowl of ice water to put them in when they're done.

4. Bring a fresh pan of water to a simmer. Add the beansprouts and cook for 1–2 minutes, then drain.

5. Cook the noodles according to the instructions. Drain and divide between two deep bowls. Then assemble the rest of the ingredients: divide the broth between the two bowls; add the chicken, beansprouts and spring onions on top; peel the eggs, cut them in half and place them on the top of the dish. Serve immediately.

AVOCADO SUSHI ROLLS

The term "sushi" refers to rice that's seasoned with vinegar, and the fillings and toppings of each piece can range from fish to vegetables to seaweed. There are many different types of sushi, but here is a recipe for one of the most iconic: the sushi roll. This recipe is for *hosomaki*, a small sushi roll with one filling.

Ingredients

90 g short-grain rice

110 ml cold water

1 ½ tbsp rice vinegar

1 tbsp sugar

½ tsp salt

3 sheets nori cut to 20 × 9 cm

Avocado, peeled, stoned and cut into strips

Soy sauce, to serve

Fukujinzuke (pickles), to serve

Note: Ideally you'd use a bamboo sushi rolling mat for this recipe, but if you don't have one, you can use a clean tea towel lined with cling film.

Method

1. To prepare the rice, follow step one on page 93.

2. Meanwhile, mix the vinegar, sugar and salt in a small pan over a medium heat until the sugar has dissolved. Once the rice has steamed, fluff it up with a wooden spoon and pour the vinegar mixture over it, then wait until the rice has cooled to room temperature.

3. Place a nori sheet on the bamboo mat, long side closest to you. Wet your hands, then press a third of the rice into a thin layer on the sheet, leaving about an inch of space clear at the top. Arrange a third of the avocado across the middle. Then take the edge of the mat and roll the sushi over the filling. Gently shape the sushi with your hands by tightening and squeezing the mat.

4. Unroll the mat, place the roll on a chopping board and cut it individual rolls with a sharp, wet knife. Repeat until all of the ingredients are used up. Serve immediately with soy sauce and pickles on the side, or pack into an airtight container and refrigerate until needed. Consume within a day.

YASAI YAKISOBA *(Serves 2)*

"Yaki" is Japanese for "fried", and "soba" are the variety of noodles in this dish, so this dish is as it sounds: noodles, swiftly stir-fried. Throw in your favourite vegetables along with a sweet-and-savoury *yakisoba* sauce, and you have a quick and delicious weeknight dinner. If you want a dish with more bite, you can substitute the soba noodles for thicker udon noodles.

Ingredients

For the yakisoba:

2 carrots

6 large mushrooms

250 g napa cabbage

100 g beansprouts

2 tbsp sesame oil

2 sheets soba noodles

Sesame seeds, to serve

For the sauce:

2 tbsp Worcester sauce

2 tbsp oyster sauce

1 tsp ketchup

1 tsp light soy sauce

1 tsp dark soy sauce

1 tsp rice vinegar

½ tsp sugar, to taste

Method

1. Prepare the vegetables: peel and slice the carrots into sticks, roughly chop the mushrooms, shred the cabbage, wash and strain the beansprouts.

2. Mix all the sauce ingredients together in a small pan and heat gently for a few minutes, until the sugar has dissolved. Adjust to taste and set aside.

3. Heat the sesame oil in a large pan on a medium-high heat. Add all the vegetables and stir-fry for 2–3 minutes.

4. Meanwhile, cook the noodles according to the packet instructions. When done, drain and add these to the frying pan along with the *yakisoba* sauce. Stir-fry for another minute, then divide between two bowls, top with sesame seeds and serve.

DAIFUKU (MOCHI)

Daifuku is a kind of *mochi,* one of the traditional sweets (*wagashi*) served during the tea ceremony. Small and round, these treats are traditionally made from *mochigome* – a kind of glutinous short-grain rice – which is steamed, pounded into a paste, then moulded into shape, and often filled with *anko*, a sweet bean paste.

Preparing the *mochigome* traditionally is a lengthy process, and it takes both time and expertise. However, there is an easier version that you can make in your own kitchen with *mochiko*, a glutinous sweet rice flour. If you can't find these ingredients in a supermarket, they can be purchased online.

Daifuku recipe *(Makes approx. 14)*

Method

1. Take a teaspoon of red bean paste at a time, roll it into a ball and set aside.

2. Add the rice flour and sugar to a heatproof bowl and whisk until combined. Continue to whisk the mixture while adding the water. Whisk quickly so that lumps don't form. If using food colouring, add it a drop at a time at this stage and mix until you reach the desired shade.

3. Cover the bowl loosely with a microwave-safe plate and microwave for 1 minute (or two minutes, if your microwave is low wattage). Then stir it and microwave again in 30-second increments until the *mochiko* dough is shiny, gelatinous and stretchy.

4. Prepare a surface with cornflour. As soon as the dough is cool enough to handle, take pieces of the dough approximately the size of 1 tbsp, coat it in cornflour and then roll it into a ball. Flatten the ball with the palm of your hand, put one ball of red bean paste in the middle, then fold the mochi dough over the red bean paste to form a ball. Repeat this until all the dough has been used.

5. Serve immediately, or store in the fridge in an airtight container and consume within two days.

Ingredients

150 g red bean paste, chilled

120 g *mochiko* (glutinous sweet rice flour)

60 g sugar

210 ml water

Gel food colouring, optional

120 g cornflour

茶の湯

Chanoyu

The tea ceremony

THE TEA CEREMONY

The Japanese tea ceremony is the ritual of preparing and serving tea for guests – a practice that's hundreds of years old, and an integral part of Japanese culture.

The ceremony itself is formal and characterized by an atmosphere of tranquillity and respect. It is usually conducted in a small room with simple but meaningful decoration, carefully chosen by the host – for instance, a sparse flower arrangement in a tall, narrow vase (*chabana*) to evoke a certain feeling or memory, or a hanging scroll showing a painting or calligraphy (*kakejiku*) which alludes to a season, or to a meaningful subject.

Before they enter the room, guests wash their hands to cleanse themselves of the outside world. They then take off their shoes and enter the tea room, usually by way of a small door, which requires guests to stoop – symbolizing humility. The guests kneel on the floor, traditionally in order of prestige, and the host will then enter. A sweet (*wagashi*) is often served, or even a meal if it is a longer ceremony.

Using choreographed motions, the host cleans each tea utensil with water and then prepares a bowl of tea. It is passed to the first guest, who will rotate the bowl to avoid drinking from the front, take a sip and then compliment the host on the tea. The guest then wipes the rim clean with a cloth, and the bowl is passed to the next guest.

There are opportunities during the ceremony for the guests to admire the utensils and the decorations of the room, and to ask questions about them, which shows respect to the host. Depending on the formality of the occasion, the ceremony could last for up to four hours.

HARMONY, PEACE AND PURITY

Although the tea ceremony might appear to be simple, there are many layers to it. It is deeply connected to the philosophy of Zen Buddhism, so the ceremony is a spiritual experience for those who take part. Through the simplicity of the decor and the meditative process of preparing and drinking tea, the guests can achieve a feeling of purity and serenity.

Chanoyu also aims to create a feeling of harmony and peace between the people who have gathered together. The ceremony is about the shared experience of giving and receiving tea, so each member in the room treats the others with respect and care, whether they are serving or being served.

It's also about showing hospitality. Each tea ceremony is a unique occasion, and everything is done with the well-being of the guests in mind. The host will have taken great care to choose a *chabana* and *kakejiku* that will best reflect the season and the theme of that particular ceremony. This attention to detail is also applied to the ceramics – which will be picked to suit each guest personally – and the utensils for preparing the tea – which will be arranged in a way that will look the most pleasing from the perspective of the guest. Every movement, even down to the host's posture and breathing, is done with intention and grace, and in the way that will be the most beautiful.

A sense of *wabi* simplicity is also present in the tea ceremony. It lies in the tea room's modest furnishing and in the contemplation that goes into the simple act of holding a cup and drinking tea. It is also present in the way that guests are able to step away from the materialistic world and find contentment in existing humbly, even if it's just for a short period of time.

WA KEI SEI JAKU

The tea ceremony is founded on four key principles: harmony, respect, purity and tranquillity – *wa kei sei jaku.*

WA

Wa is living harmoniously alongside nature and the people around you. Sharing tea is communal, so *wa* can be realized in the interaction between the host and the guest.

KEI

Kei is respect for the tea ceremony, the utensils used and the people around you, and it stems from a feeling of gratitude. *Kei* is also something that we receive in return when we show this humility and kindness to others.

SEI

Sei refers to purity that is both physical and spiritual. It is the cleanliness and organization of the tea room, and it is also a purity of the heart – the ability to treat others with a complete kindness and lack of judgement. To be pure does not mean to be perfect, but to be natural and true.

JAKU

Jaku is a level of complete stillness and tranquillity of the mind and spirit, which can only be achieved after practising and fully embodying the other three principles.

Although these four qualities are the foundations of the tea ceremony, they are still valuable outside the tea room. By applying these principles to the everyday, we can each live a peaceful life with an open and grateful heart, and also bring kindness to the lives of others.

When you hear the splash of the water drops that fall into the stone bowl you will feel that all the dust of your mind is washed away.

Sen no Rikyū on the tea ceremony

INSPIRED BY THE TEA CEREMONY

There are many ways that we can be inspired by the tea ceremony to find moments of peace and harmony in our day-to-day lives.

Be mindful as you complete simple everyday tasks, and carry them out with care. When you're preparing food, use smooth, deliberate movements to slice and chop; note the textures and colours of different ingredients, and the delicious aroma of the meal you're creating. Or, perhaps, if you are making a cup of tea or coffee, focus on the actions of pouring the water and the motion of stirring, and give your full attention to the very first sip.

Perhaps a catch-up with friends could also be inspired by the tea ceremony's peaceful ritual. When you have people coming over, think about the presentation of the room that you will gather in – ensure that it's tidy, and consider adding flourishes to the room to personalize it, such as flowers, photos or candles. Prepare with your guests in mind – whether it's stocking up on a particular kind of drink or snack that they enjoy, or having a blanket or extra cushions at the ready – and aim to make them feel as welcome and comfortable as possible.

一期一会

ICHI-GO ICHI-E

(ih-chee-goh-ih-chee-eh)

*A word originating from the tea
ceremony: every moment is special
because it only happens once.*

温泉

Onsen

Hot springs and bathing

VISITING THE *ONSEN*

In Japan, the act of bathing stands for more than just the process of getting clean. For thousands of years, visiting an *onsen* has been an opportunity for socializing, connecting to others and, most of all, relaxation.

Onsen are natural hot springs, and Japan's abundance of volcanoes means that they bubble up all over the country. These geothermal pools occur amid incredible landscapes, and bathers are often surrounded by a natural vista of mountains, clouds, forests and gardens as they bathe in the mineral-rich waters.

Visiting baths as a group is still a popular pastime today for those who seek a tranquil atmosphere and respite from the daily grind. The Buddhist monks who first incorporated the *onsen* into their rituals bathed to purify both the body and spirit, and this philosophy still exists today. Bathing is a restorative activity and a chance to take time out of the day to slow down and relax.

Spending time in the *onsen* is also a chance to connect to others, particularly because the custom is to bathe completely naked. Free from the trappings of clothes and status, the hierarchies of normal life are suspended for a short time; you are equal to every other bather around you. Attending the baths with a friend, family member or even a colleague will often deepen your relationship, because you share an experience of vulnerability, trust and equality together.

BATHING AT HOME

In a Japanese home, you are likely to find the bathroom fitted with an *ofuro* – a Japanese-style bath. Traditionally, *ofuro* are made of wood, and they tend to be deeper than a Western-style bath, allowing you to sink into the steamy water right up to your neck.

Whether you are bathing in an *onsen* or in the comfort of your own home, in an *ofuro*, the same steps will apply to the bathing process: first, you must clean yourself, taking care to get rid of any soap suds from your body. In an *onsen*, there will often be a shower area with a row of low taps. Bathers sit on a stool and wash themselves by sluicing bowls of water over their bodies. Traditionally, a Japanese bathroom is built like a wet room, so bathers will use the same technique at home, by pouring water over themselves. Only once your body is clean can you enter the bath. Then simply sit and soak for as long as you want, and allow your mind and body to unwind.

Bathing at home is a ritual just as much as it is in the *onsen*. Even the word itself gives an idea of the prestige that bathing holds; "*furo*" is the word for the bath, and the preceding "*o*" is an honorific, imbuing the act of bathing with significance and respect.

居心地が良い

IGOKOCHI GA YOI

(ee-goh-koh-chee-gah-yoh-ee)

Translates to mean that where you are makes your heart happy, or that you feel completely at home where you are.

A JAPANESE-INSPIRED BATH

We often treat washing, showering or bathing as just one more task to complete in our busy days – but it needn't be such a chore. Take inspiration from the Japanese way of bathing and create a bath-time experience to savour and enjoy.

1. CLEAN YOURSELF

Wash your body before you get into the bath and make sure you clean all the soapy residue before you bathe. You could do this by having a separate shower before you run your bath. This way, when you soak you will not be sitting in dirty water.

2. HOT WATER

Run the bath water hot. To qualify as an *onsen,* water must be at least 25°C but is often much higher. Water in an *ofuro* tends to be run between 38 and 43°C – slightly hotter than body temperature. As well as being soothing, the heat can improve circulation, relieve muscle pain and help you to sleep better. However, be careful not to run the water hotter than you are comfortable with, and keep the temperature lower if you have any health conditions that could be affected by the heat.

3. BATH SALTS

Indulge yourself by adding your favourite bath salts. Like the water in an *onsen,* bath salts contain many beneficial minerals which will be absorbed into your skin. They also add colour and a relaxing fragrance to your bath, transforming it into a luxurious spa-like experience. Alternatively, include some essential oils by adding citrus fruit peels to the water.

4. DRESS FOR COMFORT

When you have finished, change into your comfiest clothes and enjoy the sleepy warm-and-soft feeling that the bath will have left you with.

家計簿

Kakeibo

Budgeting and saving money

KAKEIBO

This is bookkeeping – streamlined. Using nothing more than pen and paper, a *kakeibo* (a "household finance ledger") helps you to take stock of your budget, to understand your spending habits and to save money.

The method was popularized by Hani Motoko, Japan's first female journalist. She believed that happiness was largely dependent on your financial stability, so, to help families live better lives, she published the first *kakeibo* in a women's magazine in 1904. It has since helped countless households across the country – and now the world – to tidy up their finances.

The technique is simple but effective, and it's an uncomplicated way to feel in control of

your money. As well as helping you to see the big picture of your outgoings, it allows you to prioritize what really matters to you. As a result, using a *kakeibo* brings an element of mindfulness to your accounts.

The fact that it must be done with a pen and paper is also significant. Most of our money is intangible, rarely passing through our hands and existing only by way of credit and debit cards, so not only is there something comforting about using a pen and paper to bring a touch of reality back to your finances, but a paper ledger, as opposed to a digital one, engages your thought processes and helps you to absorb information more easily.

HOW TO USE A *KAKEIBO*

The *kakeibo* method helps you to keep track of what you spend, a month at a time, by asking you to categorize each transaction. By the end of the month, you will have a comprehensive picture of how much of your income you spend and how you spend it.

You will need an A4 piece of paper per month of expenditure. Alternatively, invest in a notebook specifically for bookkeeping. That way, all your records will be in one place.

The method is made up of four questions:

HOW MUCH MONEY DO YOU HAVE?

Take an A4 piece of paper, or page of your notebook. At the top, write down your monthly income, minus all the fixed costs, such as rent and monthly bills.

HOW MUCH ARE YOU SPENDING?

Divide your paper up into four columns, one with each of the following headings:

- **Survival**: regular, necessary expenditure, such as food, childcare and transport costs.
- **Culture**: expenditure on cultural activities, theatre, books, the cinema, museums or magazines.

- **Optional**: anything you choose to spend money on, like having dinner out, social events, shopping or takeaways.
- **Extra**: anything irregular or unexpected, such as birthday cards/presents or repairs around the house.

Over the next month, record everything you spend in the relevant column, no matter how small. Try to be as realistic as you can; for instance, it may feel like you *needed* that new top or that cup of coffee, but it's more likely that these would count as "optional" spends rather than "survival". At the end of the month, take stock of your outgoings. How does it compare to your monthly income? Are you spending significantly more in one area than another?

HOW MUCH MONEY DO YOU WANT TO SAVE?

Do you want to go on a holiday? Or would you simply like to have some spare money left over at the end of the month? Think about where you would like to be and set yourself achievable goals.

Remember to think about how you will achieve these goals too. Look at the areas where you spend the most and try to identify areas where you can cut costs. Perhaps you can pack your own lunch instead of buying it out, or visit charity shops to find second-hand books, clothes and films to enjoy, rather than always buying brand new.

HOW CAN YOU IMPROVE?

This is more of a question to start asking yourself once you have two or three months' data to hand. Have you achieved your savings goals? If not, investigate why this is. Is the goal unrealistic, or is there an area where you're still overspending? Make a new goal for the following month, making a change either to your savings goal or to your spending habits. On the other hand, if you have reached your goal, are you happy with this or do you want to save more?

Total income per month: £1200
Income minus fixed costs: £540

MONTH: JUNE

SURVIVAL		CULTURE		OPTIONAL		EXTRA	
Food shop	£42.35	Cinema	£11.95	Dinner out	£23.27	B-day card	£2.50
Bus fare	£3.50			Work drinks	£18.50		
Food shop	£13.20			New dress	£19.99		

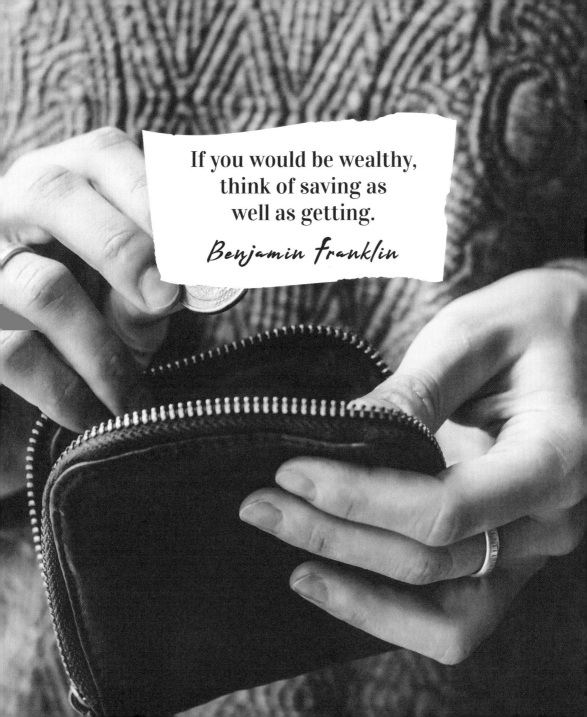

If you would be wealthy,
think of saving as
well as getting.

Benjamin Franklin

頑張って

GANBATTE

(GAN-BAH-tay)

A word of encouragement meaning a combination of "Do your best", "You can do it" and "Give it your best shot!" Where we might wish someone "Good luck", a Japanese person might say ganbatte!

生け花

Ikebana

The art of flower arranging

IKEBANA

Many people think of *ikebana* as the art of arranging flowers. While this is technically correct, the translation of the word gives us a much more nuanced picture: *ikebana* means "living flowers" or "giving life to flowers". This translation suggests that there are hidden depths contained within the arrangements, and it hints at a deep connection between the artist and the plants that they work with – it tells us that *ikebana* is richer and more complex than it first appears.

The plants and flowers used in an *ikebana* arrangement will usually be simple, seasonal and asymmetrical. Most arrangements will have a tall branch or stem as the background, which acts as a defining line of the composition. In front of this will be the main focus of the arrangement, a plant that naturally draws your eye and brings the elements together – usually a flower or a striking array of leaves. Then, smaller elements such as foliage, stems or flowers will fill the space around the base of the arrangement.

There are many different styles of *ikebana*, and depending on which school of thought the artist belongs to, there may be further rules determining how the arrangements should be put together – the height of each branch or flower, the angle they're placed at or the number of elements that each arrangement can have.

However, no matter what methodology is used, *ikebana* arrangements are more than the sum of their parts. Through the skill of the artist, ordinary materials are elevated and bestowed with the power to express many feelings, ideas and emotions. The stark wood of a bare branch combined with other sparse plants might evoke winter or a sense of solemnity, whereas the freshness and vitality of brightly coloured flowers amid lush green leaves might suggest spring, or a feeling of energy.

BEAUTY IN IMPERFECTION

All elements of a plant can be used in an *ikebana* arrangement: seeds, leaves, pods, flowers, stems and branches. Each one can add its own layer of meaning to the finished piece, especially if they are weathered or aged. For instance, a withered leaf or a branch covered with moss can imbue an arrangement with a sense of *wabi sabi* – the idea that life is always changing and that poignant beauty can be found in imperfection.

Each arrangement will be unique, because every plant has its own individual shape and qualities. The artist's skill is to see these traits and arrange the plants in a way that emphasizes them and allows them to speak.

Happiness is to hold
flowers in both hands.

Japanese proverb

THE PEACEFUL NATURE OF *IKEBANA*

There are many benefits to practising *ikebana*. It's a way to express yourself, as you can convey any feeling, idea or memory through your selection of plants and flowers. It's also creative but with the comfort of boundaries; you are restricted by the materials you have, so *ikebana* could almost be described as a puzzle, as you need to take the time to discover the optimal way to piece the plants together.

It also helps your thoughts to become still. Similar to meditation, a mind practising *ikebana* needs to be relaxed but also focused, and the concentration you pour into your arrangement makes it an immersive pastime. As such, this art form is a wonderful way to quieten your mind and find a sense of peace amid a busy life.

Perhaps most of all, *ikebana* is about strengthening your connection to nature. Like bonsai, *ikebana* arrangements aim to imitate the natural world at the same time as being highly cultivated; they are a convergence between what is wild and what is human. By practising *ikebana* – spending time with natural materials, being sensitive to them and giving them enough time and attention to find the best way to display them – we bring ourselves closer to the natural world.

花の心

HANA-NO-KOKORO

(hah-nah-noh-koh-koh-roh)

Meaning "flower heart", this is a particular sensitivity needed to truly master the art of ikebana. It describes a kind of communication whereby your own heart is open to the heart of the flower and that there is a feeling of true understanding between the two.

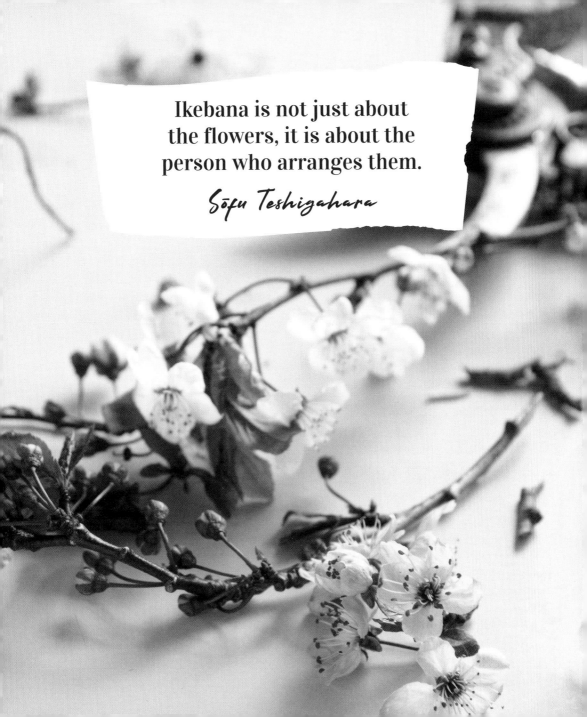

Ikebana is not just about the flowers, it is about the person who arranges them.

Sōfu Teshigahara

IKEBANA INSPIRATION

Here are a few tips on creating your own *ikebana*-inspired arrangements.

You will need:

- A container
- A *kenzan* (see opposite)
- Plant materials
- Scissors
- String or wire

SETTING UP

Choose a container. It could be shallow and bowl-like or a tall vase. Think about the kind of arrangement you want to create and which colour and style of container will best express this. You will also need a *kenzan* (also known as a "flower frog"), a metal plate with spikes sticking up out of it. It is placed at the bottom of the container and is used to hold the flowers in place. These can be purchased cheaply online.

FLORA AND FAUNA

If you have a garden, it's likely that you will already have everything you need for your own *ikebana*-style arrangement. Search the natural environments near you for leaves, branches, stems, flowers and foliage, and pick out elements that attract you (although if you take any cuttings, ensure you have permission from the landowner). Alternatively, you could visit a flower shop. For a simple arrangement, you will need three types of plant material: a plant that will stand tall and create height, a plant for the middle of the composition to draw the eye and material to balance the bottom of the arrangement.

THE ARRANGEMENT

First, put the *kenzan* in the bottom of your container and cover it with water. Then place your tallest element. Add the remaining elements in descending height order. Take your time and experiment with placements, angles and heights until you find an arrangement that you are happy with and which expresses the feeling you want to convey. You may want to use your string/ wire to secure plants in place. When you are finished, place your arrangement against a plain background so that the lines you have created stand out and can be given the full attention they deserve.

Kenzan

盆
栽

Bonsai

The art of growing small trees

BONSAI

Bonsai is the art of growing and cultivating miniature trees. Most of us will be familiar with these distinctive plants, which seem at once both natural and refined – tiny branches presenting immaculate pads of leaves, trunks that appear gnarled with age and their twisted silhouettes giving the illusion that they have been growing in the wild for hundreds of years. With *bon* meaning "basin" or "tray", and *sai* meaning "to plant", the word bonsai translates roughly as "tree planted in a shallow container". But there is much more to these compact trees than meets the eye. A bonsai is no mere pot plant – it is a living art form.

Growing a bonsai tree takes many years of painstaking care, dedication and patience; it can take between three and five years before a tree grown from a seedling can even begin to be styled, and even then it could be another ten years before the tree is considered mature enough to be shown. For this reason, these plants are highly treasured and will be passed down from generation to generation.

Throughout a bonsai's life, its roots will be trimmed routinely to keep it healthy in its shallow container. Strong wire will be wrapped around the trunk and branches to encourage them to grow into particular shapes. As it matures, the branches will be pruned to keep the tree in the artist's desired shape. Leaves will be trimmed and shaped selectively to keep the overall silhouette neat and tidy. Sometimes trees will even be defoliated: all the leaves will be removed, allowing smaller leaves to grow back in their place, which creates a denser image overall.

THE GIFTS OF BONSAI

There are numerous rewards for those who work with bonsai trees. Many would say that, primarily, the art form strengthens your connection to nature. While you can bring your own ideas to your bonsai – such as where its branches and leaves will be – you cannot truly impose yourself on it. Instead, you are shaping it, working with it and fusing your own ideas with the soul of the tree. Similar to the sensitivity you develop while practising *ikebana*, the awareness that you are working *with* rather than *on* the tree forges that close connection to the natural world.

It also helps you to slow down. Working on a bonsai is a long process that requires time, patience and no small amount of focus; each change you make to the tree must be implemented with care, and progress is so incremental that it's nearly impossible to see unless you stick with it for months or years. The ability to accept this gradual pace brings you a sense of calm and peacefulness.

If you are interested in trying your hand at cultivating a bonsai tree, visit your local garden centre, or seek out a bonsai demonstration for more information.

風
物
詩

FUUBUTSUSHI

(FOO-boo-tsoo-shee)

Something that reminds you
of a particular season.

BONSAI COMPANION

Bonsai tend to live for as long as they are looked after – the oldest is thought to be over 1,000 years old – so, if cared for properly, your bonsai can be with you for the span of your whole life. You will spend hours contemplating the plant, caring for it and nurturing it, and it will grow and change as you also grow and change. It's a living example of your dedication and care. After you have spent many years with it, you, your life and your memories are inside the bonsai tree as much as the calm spirit of the bonsai is within you.

Your bonsai is always beside
you, and it accumulates
time filled with memories.

Chiako Yamamoto

ENJOYING BONSAI

Bonsai trees are made to be seen, and there is just as much to be gained from viewing and considering them as there is from cultivating them.

Bonsai are a calming and comforting presence, and spending time with these trees helps you to find a sense of stillness within yourself. They can also inspire a sense of awe and reverence. When you view a bonsai, consider the care and patience that has gone into creating it: that even the smallest trees take years to grow, and that everything about it will have been considered, right down to the individual leaves or needles.

Bonsai trees are also evocative, and they are designed to inspire an emotional response in the viewer. Their miniature forms imitate a tree that has grown in the wild, but the human hand is able to add layers of meaning, so a bonsai tree will always signify something more than itself. From the shape of the bonsai – whether it's upright, cascading over the edge of the pot or slanting to one side as if it's being blown in the wind – to the shape and colour of the pot, the trees can convey seasons, a feeling or a theme such as life, death or resilience. It's up to the viewer to absorb the tree and to allow it to suggest ideas of the wider world.

PERFECTLY IMPERFECT

Bonsai trees are often imbued with a sense of *wabi sabi*. The artist must accept the idea that it is impermanent – cultivating a bonsai tree is a continuous work; it will always be changing and it will never be finished. It can only be what it is in the present moment.

For the viewer, the beauty of the bonsai is often found in it's imperfections. The bark will appear weathered; the shape of the tree will often include bends and turns; the composition will be asymmetrical. It is these elements that give the tree the impression of history, experience and age and allow it to suggest the feeling of something larger than itself.

The object is not to make the tree look like a bonsai, but to make the bonsai look like a tree.

John Naka

折り紙

Origami

The art of paper folding

ORIGAMI

Although paper folding is not exclusive to Japan, it was the Japanese who elevated it into the art form we know today as origami.

In its early history, origami was practised only by the elite because paper was scarce, and it tended to be reserved for religious purposes. However, during the seventeenth and eighteenth centuries, when the paper industry began to flourish, origami quickly became more widespread, more decorative and more elaborate.

Today, there are many different styles of origami which are enjoyed by adults and children alike. As it requires quiet concentration, it's a calming activity to take part in, and it gives your mind a chance to change tack and to focus on something totally separate from your worries. It's also satisfying: with the simple act of folding a humble piece of paper, you can create a beautiful piece of art. Read on to learn how to fold a few origami figures of your own.

SIMPLE ORIGAMI HEART

Follow the steps below to create a simple origami heart. You will need one sheet of origami paper, or any sheet of paper cut to 7.5x7.5 cm (3x3 in).

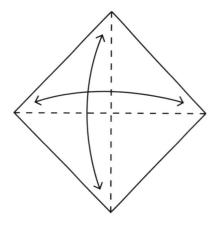

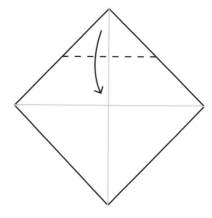

1. Take a square of paper, in a colour of your choice, and fold along the diagonals to make crease lines.

2. Fold the top corner to the middle of the paper.

3. Take hold of the bottom corner and fold it up to meet the folded top of the paper.

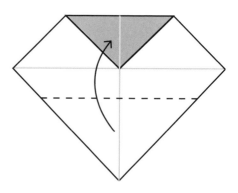

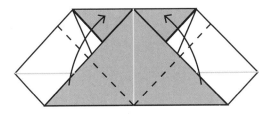 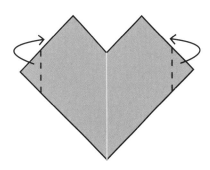

4. Take the right-hand corner and fold it upward so that it's in line with the centre fold on your paper. Do the same with the left-hand corner.

5. Fold the two outer corners of the paper inward, away from you.

6. Finally, fold over the top corners to create the top of the heart.

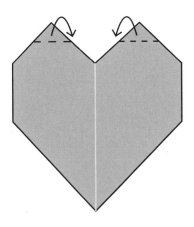 

BUTTERFLY

Follow the steps below to create a beautiful origami butterfly. You will need one sheet of origami paper, or any sheet of paper cut to 7.5x7.5 cm (3x3 in).

1. Fold a square of paper in half and then unfold it again, so you are left with a crease down the middle. Rotate it 90 degrees and do the same, then do the same for both diagonals. When you've finished, you should have a square of paper with crease lines in a star shape. Then fold the paper in half again. As you fold, push the sides inward to form a triangle shape.

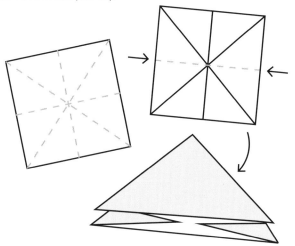

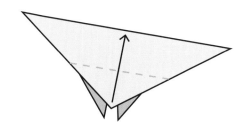

2. Your triangle will have two layers. Take the left-hand corner from the top layer of the triangle and fold it upward so it's in line with the centre fold. Do the same with the top right-hand corner.

3. Turn the paper over so that the triangle tip is facing toward you. Take the tip and begin to fold it upward. You will begin to make a diamond shape.

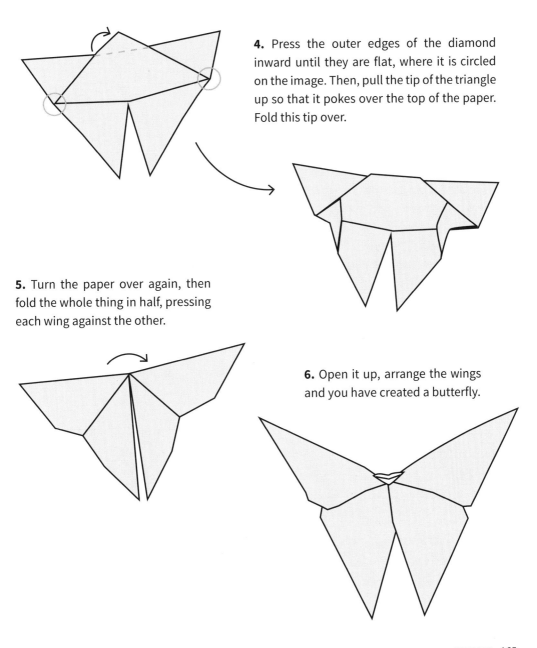

4. Press the outer edges of the diamond inward until they are flat, where it is circled on the image. Then, pull the tip of the triangle up so that it pokes over the top of the paper. Fold this tip over.

5. Turn the paper over again, then fold the whole thing in half, pressing each wing against the other.

6. Open it up, arrange the wings and you have created a butterfly.

CRANE

Cranes are auspicious in Japanese culture, symbolizing happiness, good fortune and eternal youth, so they are both a traditional and popular origami figure to master. Ancient legends tell that cranes can live for 1,000 years, and that any person who can fold 1,000 paper cranes will be granted a wish by the gods. After World War II, cranes also became a symbol of peace and healing, and they are often left at memorials and monuments as a sign of respect.

Follow the steps below to create a traditional origami crane. You will need one sheet of origami paper, or any sheet of paper cut to 7.5x7.5 cm (3x3 in).

1. Take the paper and fold the top corner to the bottom corner.

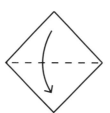

2. Now fold the left corner over to the right corner.

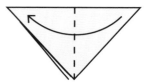

3. Open the top flap and fold the top corner to meet the bottom corner; then flip over and do the same on the other side.

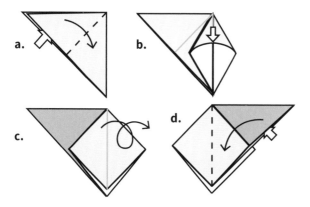

a.

b.

c.

d.

4. On the top layer, fold the left and right corners to meet in the centre and fold down the top triangle. Then turn the paper over and do the same on the other side.

5. Unfold step 4 and open up the top layer. Using the creases as guides, fold the left and right sides into the centre. Turn the paper over and repeat with the other side.

6. You will have a diamond shape. Take the outer right- and left-hand corners and fold them so that the tips meet in the centre. Turn the paper over and repeat on the other side.

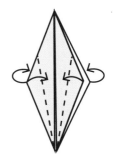

7. The wide, triangular top will become the wings of the crane, and the two thin flaps at the bottom will be the head and tail. Take the left-hand flap and fold it 180 degrees, clockwise, so that it sits between the wings. Then take the right-hand flap and fold it 180 degrees anti-clockwise, until it also sits between the wings.

8. Pull each wing outwards – this will open up the base of the paper structure so it can stand up. Then take one of the thin flaps and fold it in on itself to create the bird's head. Adjust the tail if needed – and you have created a crane.

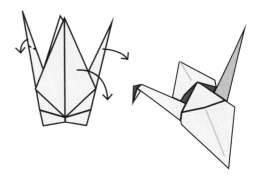

KIRIGAMI

Kirigami is another form of paper art that's similar to origami, but it involves cutting as well as folding the paper. We will probably all have tried our hand at making a paper chain of people when we were younger, or a paper snowflake – these are both examples of kirigami. Here's how to make a simple piece of decorative art – try hanging it from the ceiling or decorating a window with it. You will need one sheet of paper cut into a circle. It can be any size – but the bigger your sheet, the bigger your decoration will be.

1. Take a piece of circular paper and fold it in half to make a semi-circle. Then fold the semi-circle in half. Then fold the paper in half a third time. You should be left with a shape that looks like a slice of pizza.

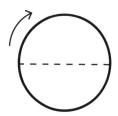 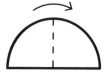

2. Draw the following design onto the paper. Make sure the side with the flower detail is the side with the main fold, then cut along the lines.

3. Gently unfold the paper. Stick it in place using sticky tack, or turn it into a hanging ornament by using a needle to run a thin thread through the top.

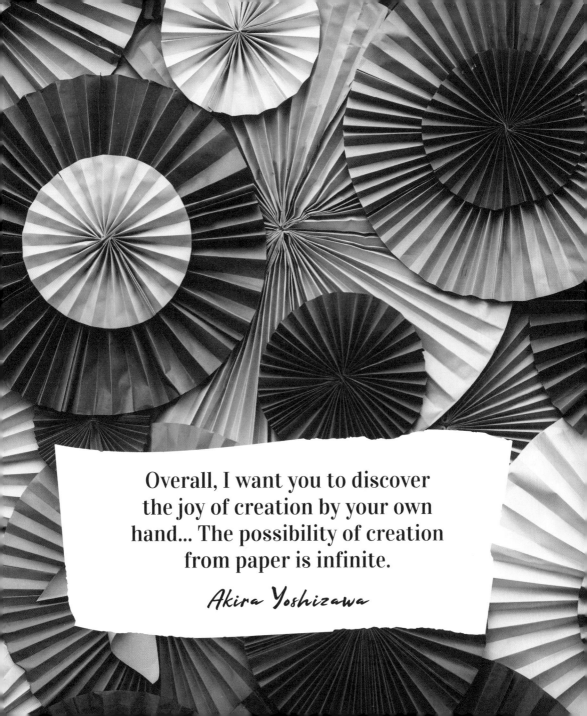

Overall, I want you to discover
the joy of creation by your own
hand... The possibility of creation
from paper is infinite.

Akira Yoshizawa

CONCLUSION

Whether you look to the philosophy of *wabi sabi*, choose to pursue your *ikigai* or focus on the wisdom of *kintsugi*; whether you find calm with *shinrin-yoku*, or through the ritual of bathing; or whether you seek a creative outlet in *ikebana*, origami or bonsai, engaging with Japanese ideas helps us to consider the way we live in a new light.

These ideas offer many valuable insights into finding fulfilment and peace. To lead a full life, look for beauty in the everyday and find small moments to cherish; joy lies in being grateful for the little things and in being able to focus on what is truly important. Seek out what makes your heart sing and pursue it without fear. Accept yourself as you are in this moment, because you are one of a kind and worth celebrating. Take time to connect to the natural world and enjoy the peace you can find there. Remember to pause, breathe and reflect, as this is what will restore you. And, perhaps most importantly, make the most of the time that you have, because life is short, precious and always changing.

A calm and happy life is something that we all deserve and that we can all achieve. The Japanese way of living tells us that, as long as we keep an open mind and a grateful heart, the key to that happiness is already in our hands – we just have to know to look for it.

PRONUNCIATION GUIDE

Anko (AHN-koh)

Bonsai (bon-sai)

Chabana (cha-bah-na)

Chabudai (cha-boo-dai)

Chado (CHA-doh)

Chanoyu (cha-NO-yoo)

Daifuku (DAI-foo-koo)

Denki buro (den-kee-boo-roh)

Fukujinzuke
(foo-koo-JIN-zoo-keh)

Furoshiki (foo-ROH-shih-kee)

Furusato (foo-roo-sah-toh)

Fusuma (foo-SOO-mah)

Futon (foo-TON)

Fuubutsushi (FOO-boo-tsoo-shee)

Ganbatte (GAN-BAH-tay)

Genkan (GEN-kan)

Gochisousama-deshita
(goh-chih-SOH-sama-DE-shTA)

Gohan (GOH-han)

Hana-no-kokoro
(hah-nah-noh-koh-koh-roh)

Hara hachi bu
(hah-rah-HAH-chee-bu)

Hosomaki (hoh-soh-mah-kee)

Ichi-go ichi-e
(ih-chee-goh-ih-chee-eh)

Ie (ee-eh)

Igokochi ga yoi
(ee-goh-koh-chee-gah-yoh-ee)

Ikebana (ee-keh-bah-nah)

Ikigai (ee-kee-gai)

Irasshaimase
(ee-ra-SHY-mah-seh)

Itadakimasu
(ee-tah-dah-kee-mass)

Jaku (JAH-koo)

Kakeibo (KAH-keh-boh)

Kakejiku (kah-keh-jih-koo)

Kei (ke-h)

Kenzan (ken-zan)

Kintsugi (KIN-tsu-gee)

Kirigami (kee-ree-gah-mee)

Kombu (KOM-boo)

Komorebi (koh-moh-reh-bee)

Matcha (MA-tcha)

Mochi (moh-chee)

Mochigome (moh-chee-goh-meh)

Mochiko (moh-chee-koh)

Mono no aware
(moh-noh-noh-AH-wah-reh)

Mottainai (moh-TAI-NAI)

Ofuro (O-foo-roh)

Ojamashimasu
(OH-jah-mah-shi-mass)

Okagesamade
(o-kah-geh-sah-mah-deh)

Okazu (o-KAH-zoo)

Omotenashi
(o-moh-teh-nah-shee)

Onigiri (o-nee-gee-ree)

Onsen (on-sen)

Origami (o-ree-gah-mee)

Oubaitori (o-bai-toe-ree)

Sado (sah-doh)

Sei (seh)

sento (sen-toh)

Shinrin-yoku (SHIN-RIN-yoh-koo)

Shōji (SHOH-jee)

Sushi (soo-shee)

Tabemono (tah-beh-moh-noh)

Tatami (tah-tah-mee)

Tsukemono (tsu-KEH-moh-noh)

Umeboshi (oo-meh-boh-shee)

Wa (wah)

Wabi sabi (wah-bee-sah-bee)

Wagashi (wah-gah-shee)

Yakisoba (yah-kee-soh-bah)

Yasai (yah-sai)

Yūgen (YOO-gen)

Zabuton (za-BOO-ton)

IMAGE CREDITS

If you're interested in finding out more about our books, find us on Facebook at **Summersdale Publishers** and follow us on Twitter at **@Summersdale**.

www.summersdale.com